D1203861

MAKE MONEY!
HAVE A LEMONADE STAND

Bridget Heos **Illustrated by Daniele Fabbri**

Amicus Illustrated is published by Amicus
P.O. Box 1329, Mankato, MN 56002
www.amicuspublishing.us

Library of Congress Cataloging-in-Publication Data
Heos, Bridget.
 Make money! Have a lemonade stand / by Bridget
Heos ; illustrated by Daniele Fabbri.
     pages cm. — (Make money!)
 Summary: "Through trial and error and few humorous
mistakes, a girl learns how to make her lemonade stand
successful and earn enough money for the toy she
wants"—Provided by publisher.
 ISBN 978-1-60753-361-0 (library binding) —
ISBN 978-1-60753-409-9 (ebook)
1. Vending stands—Juvenile literature. 2. Lemonade—
Juvenile literature. 3. Money—making projects for
children—Juvenile literature. I. Fabbri, Daniele, illustrator.
II. Title.
 HF5392.H46 2014
 381'.4566363—dc23
                                    2012050573

Editor: Rebecca Glaser
Designer: The Design Lab

Printed in the United States of America at
Corporate Graphics in North Mankato, Minnesota.

Date 2/2013   PO 1147

10 9 8 7 6 5 4 3 2 1

That toy is really cute. And all your friends have it. It costs $7.25. Your dad says you have to earn the money yourself. But how?

You could have a lemonade stand. Maybe a friend could help.

First, get your supplies. Ask your dad to take you to the store.

Lemonade mix and 40 cups cost $8.
How will you pay for it?
Your dad gives you a loan.

Time to make the lemonade. The more you have, the more money you'll make. What if you added TONS of water to make more?

You're probably right. That would make the lemonade taste watery. Better follow the directions instead. Mmm. Perfect!

How much will you charge? At $10 per cup, you would soon be rich. But no one will pay that much.

At 5¢ a cup, everybody will buy it. But supplies cost $8. When you divide $8 by 40 cups, it works out to 20¢ per cup. You need to charge more than that to make a profit. Try 50¢ per cup.

Now set up your table outside.
It's very quiet here. Where can you
find more customers?

Try the park. That's better.

Why isn't anybody stopping? They didn't know about the lemonade stand, so they didn't bring money. You need to advertise.

Your advertising worked! You have a line of customers. You'll need to work fast.

Whoa! Careful. You need a system so you don't spill. You can pour and serve. Your friend can take the money and make change. Don't forget to smile.

Wow. You've sold 16 cups. At 50¢ each, that adds up to $8.

Don't forget to pay your dad for the loan! Maybe tomorrow you'll make enough money for the toy.

Wednesday is windy and cloudy. It's a slow day. But look, there's a baseball game here tomorrow. Better bring extra lemonade!

You're out of lemonade. And you made $12. Time to buy that toy! But wait. Your friend did half the work. If you split the money, you'll have $6. That's not enough for the toy. And your sign says you'll be here tomorrow.

You do have enough money to buy
more lemonade. You can use $8 to buy more
lemonade and 40 more cups. Good idea.

Friday is really hot. This is your best day
yet. Wow! You're out of lemonade. You and your
friend did equal work, so you split the money.

Now you can buy the cute toy, and still have a little left over for a rainy day . . . or to buy more lemonade!

Counting Your Money!

If you start a lemonade stand, keep track of how much money you spend and how much money you make. Here's a sample based on this story.

TUESDAY	
16 cups sold at 50 cents each	$8.00
Pay back loan	− $8.00
You have left	0.00
WEDNESDAY	
0 cups sold	0.00
THURSDAY	
24 cups sold at 50 cents each	$12.00
Buy supplies for 40 cups lemonade	− $8.00
What's left	$4.00
Pay your friend half	− $2.00
You have left	$2.00
FRIDAY	
40 cups sold at 50 cents each	$20.00
Pay your friend half	− $10.00
You have left	$10.00
Your total profit for the week	$12.00

Glossary

advertise To tell customers about your business through signs or other messages.

customer A person who buys or might buy what you're selling.

loan Money given to you that you must pay back. The borrower usually pays interest (more than the original loan). Probably not when it's your dad, though.

profit Money made after expenses are paid.

supplies Items needed to make something or provide a service.

system An organized way of doing a job.

Read More

Antill, Sara. *10 Ways I Can Earn Money*. New York: PowerKids Press, 2012.

Orr, Tamra. *A Kid's Guide to Earning Money*. Hockessin, Del.: Mitchell Lane, 2009.

Scheunemann, Pam. *Cool Jobs for Super Sales Kids: Ways to Make Money Selling Stuff*. Edina, Minn.: Abdo, 2011.

Websites

Lemonade Day
http://lemonadeday.org
Join thousands of kids who are learning how to start, own, and operate a business—a lemonade stand.

PBS Kids.org: It's My Life: Money
http://pbskids.org/itsmylife/money/
Learn how to earn, save, and spend wisely.

Virtual Lemonade Stand
http://www.omsi.edu/exhibits/moneyville/activities/lemonade/lemonadestand.htm
Try this game to see if you can create a successful lemonade stand business.

About the Author

Bridget Heos is the author of more than 40 books for children, but she made her millions (of pennies) in grade school selling lemonade. She and her family live in Kansas City. You can find out more about her at www.authorbridgetheos.com.

About the Illustrator

Daniele Fabbri was born in Ravenna, Italy, in 1978. He graduated from Istituto Europeo di Design in Milan, Italy, and started his career as cartoon animator, storyboarder, and background designer for animated series. He has worked as a freelance illustrator since 2003, collaborating with international publishers and advertising agencies.